The Yoga House

Jesse Bennett

Archway Publishing books may be ordered through booksellers or by contacting:

Archway Publishing
1663 Liberty Drive
Bloomington, IN 47403
www.archwaypublishing.com
1 (888) 242-5904

ISBN: 978-1-4808-6807-6 (sc)
ISBN: 978-1-4808-6808-3 (hc)
ISBN: 978-1-4808-6806-9 (e)

Print information available on the last page.

Archway Publishing rev. date: 9/19/2018

The Yoga House

This book is dedicated to Madison and Samuel the most beautiful, magical little yogis a mama could dream to have! I love you bigger than the sky and all the stars in it and to my husband Ryan who helps make our home a yoga house!

To all the families teaching goodness and kindness to their children, thank you for making the world a brighter place!

Contents

We live in a yoga house. It is built
on love and kindness.

We share our toys.

We share our feelings.

We share our snacks.

We treat others how we hope to be treated.

We dance our wiggles out!

We use our imagination
to create and explore!

We dream big and shine bright!

SHINE
LIKE
THE
SUN

We see magic around us.
We see the magic within us.

We breathe deep to calm our mind
and our body after a busy day.

We are grateful every day for the love
around us and the love within us.

At the end of each day we think of
what made us happy, and we smile
because today was a good day.

We live in a yoga house. We let our light shine so bright! We see the good in ourselves and the good in others. We know that love is the heart of our home!

Yoga House Affirmation

I AM

I am strong

I am loved

I am special

I am kind

I make this world a beautiful place

Nighttime Guided Meditation

Breathe with me
Breathe with me like the roots in the
trees to the leaves flowing free
Breathe with me like the ocean
waves flowing in and out
Breathe with me as the sun rises
in the sky and the day wakes
Breathe with me as the birds
soar and the grass dances
Breathe with me as the sun begins
to set and the moon rises
Breathe with me as you snuggle in my arms
Let your breath soften you, calm you, and
bring you the sweetest dreams. You are the
sun, the moon, and all that is beautiful in my
world. Breathe with me sweet one, and dream
big for tomorrow is yours to make great

Yoga House Journal

What made me smile today?

Our house is filled with....

Our favorite songs to dance to ....

Our favorite games to play are...

I love it when....

Today, this is how I showed kindness...